MW01040661

DATE DUE

MAR 2 9 2002	
JAN 0 6 2004	
APR 1 1 2008	
FEB 0 5 2009	
GAYLORD	PRINTED IN U.S.A.

Smith College Campus School Library
Gill Hall
Northampton, MA 01063

IRISH IMMIGRANTS
1840-1920

by Megan O'Hara

Content Consultant:
Christopher Shannon, Associate Director
Cushwa Center for the Study of American Catholicism
Notre Dame, Indiana

Blue Earth Books

an imprint of Capstone Press
Mankato, Minnesota

Smith College Campus School Library
Gill Hall
Northampton, MA 01063

Blue Earth Books are published by Capstone Press
151 Good Counsel Drive, P.O. Box 669, Mankato, Minnesota 56002
http://www.capstone-press.com

Copyright © 2002 by Capstone Press. All rights reserved.
No part of this book may be reproduced without written permission from the publisher.
The publisher takes no responsibility for the use of any of the materials
or methods described in this book, nor for the products thereof.
Printed in the United States of America.

Library of Congress Cataloging-in-Publication Data
O'Hara, Megan.
    Irish Immigrants, 1840–1920 / by Megan O'Hara.
    p. cm. – (Coming to America)
    Includes bibliographical references (p. 31) and index.
    ISBN 0-7368-0795-0
    1. Irish Americans—History—Juvenile literature. 2. Immigrants—United States—History—Juvenile literature. 3. United States—Emigration and
immigration—History—Juvenile literature. [1. Irish Americans—History. 2. United States—Emigration and immigration.] I. Title II. Series.
E184.I6 O48 2002
973' .049162—dc21   2001000730

Summary: Discusses the reasons Irish people left their homeland to come to America, the experiences immigrants had in the new country, and the
contributions this cultural group made to American society. Includes sidebars and activities.

Editorial credits
Editor: Kay M. Olson
Designer: Heather Kindseth
Photo researchers: Heidi Schoof and Alta Schaffer
Product planning editor: Lois Wallentine

Photo credits
National Archives, cover, 20; Gregg Andersen, flag images, 8, 17;
National Library of Ireland, 4, 9, 16; Stock Montage, Inc., 6; Archive
Photos, 10; Sean Sexton Collection/CORBIS, 11; Bettmann/CORBIS,
14, 26 (left); 29 (both); Library of Congress, 13, 15, 19, 21; David J. &
Janice L. Frent Collection/CORBIS, 18; Robert Dennis Collection of
Stereoscopic Views, The New York Public Library, 23; Sandy
Felsenthal/CORBIS, 25; Capstone Press/Gary Sundermeyer, 24,
26 (right)

1 2 3 4 5 6 07 06 05 04 03 02

Contents

IRISH IMMIGRANTS 1840 TO 1920

EARLY IRISH IMMIGRANTS

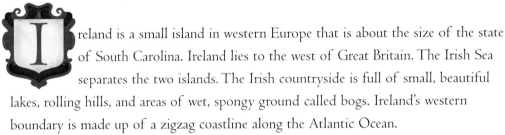

Ireland is a small island in western Europe that is about the size of the state of South Carolina. Ireland lies to the west of Great Britain. The Irish Sea separates the two islands. The Irish countryside is full of small, beautiful lakes, rolling hills, and areas of wet, spongy ground called bogs. Ireland's western boundary is made up of a zigzag coastline along the Atlantic Ocean.

Irish people have a long history of moving westward across the Atlantic Ocean to America. During the 1700s, many Irish people left the poverty and high taxes of the Ulster region in the northern part of Ireland to make their fortunes in colonial America.

The first Irish immigrants often came to America as indentured servants. They borrowed the cost of their ship passage across the Atlantic Ocean and promised to work without wages until their debt was repaid. After a few years of work, an indentured servant earned a new suit of clothes, a few simple tools, and the freedom to make a new life in the New World.

During the mid- to late-1800s, millions of Irish people left Donegal (below) and other port cities for America.

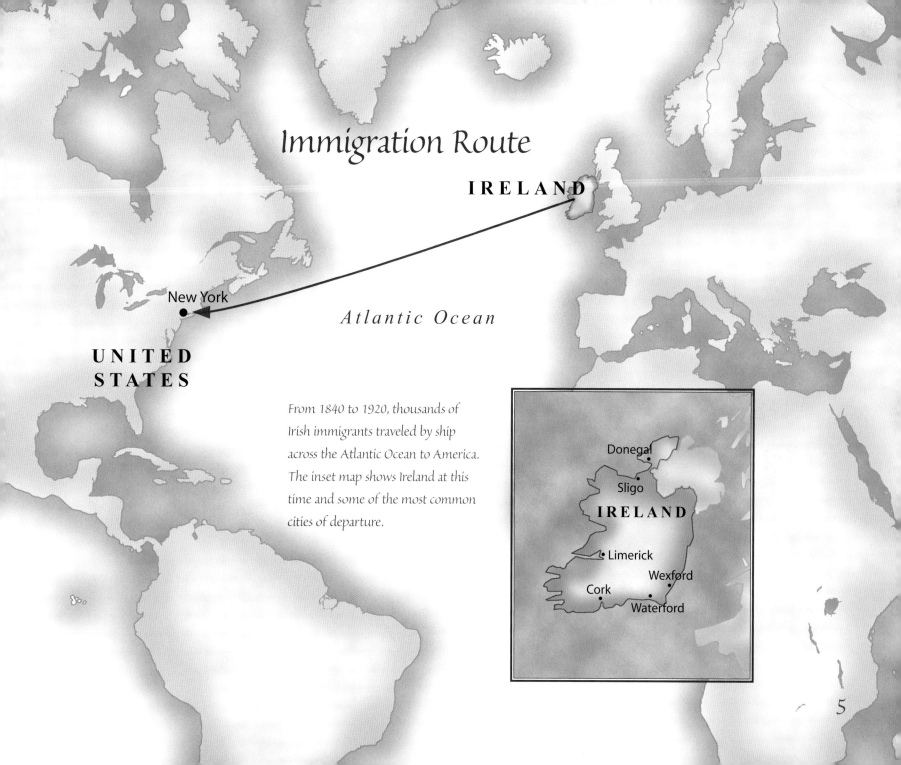

Immigration Route

IRELAND

UNITED STATES

New York

Atlantic Ocean

From 1840 to 1920, thousands of Irish immigrants traveled by ship across the Atlantic Ocean to America. The inset map shows Ireland at this time and some of the most common cities of departure.

Donegal

Sligo

IRELAND

Limerick

Wexford

Cork

Waterford

Irish peasants dug up their potato crop by hand. When the Potato Famine struck Ireland, the people had no food to eat.

In the 1800s, the steady flow of Irish immigrants traveling across the Atlantic Ocean became a flood. Between 1800 and 1844, there were a little more than 8 million people living in Ireland. During those same years, more than 600,000 Irish people left their homeland to come to the United States. Most of these immigrants were Irish Catholics from the southern and western regions of Ireland. They were poor, unskilled workers who owned no land of their own. They came to America in search of a better life.

In 1845, the Potato Famine struck Ireland. Almost overnight, a fungus attacked potato crops in the Irish fields. Few healthy potatoes were left to use for planting the next year's crop. For five years in a row, the potato crops in Ireland failed. The worst year of the blight came in 1847, which sometimes is called Black '47.

The Potato Famine left Irish peasants without the means to survive. They always had used part of their potato crop to pay the rent on their land. With no way to pay the landowners, peasants were forced out of their homes. Families lived under bridges, in caves, or beside roads. Everywhere in Ireland, people were dying of starvation or disease.

Irish immigration to America continued throughout the 1800s and early 1900s. Between 1841 and 1850, about 780,700 Irish people left Ireland for America and Canada. By the late 1800s, so many people had died or left Ireland that the country's population dropped to 4 million. From 1820 to 1920, more than 4.5 million people emigrated and left Ireland. Today, 40 million Americans can claim that one or more of their ancestors came from Ireland.

Grow Potatoes in a Pot

You can grow potatoes even if you do not have garden space. Use a large flowerpot, a clean plastic pail, or a large tub. Grow your pot potatoes on a sunny porch, driveway, or patio balcony. You should be able to harvest enough potatoes to make hashbrowns or another potato sidedish for a family meal.

What You Need

a large pot or planting container about
    24 inches (60 centimeters) in diameter
knife
garden earth or potting soil

pot saucer
one potato with six to eight "eyes"
ruler
watering can or hose

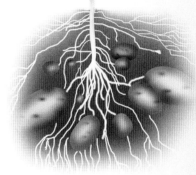

What You Do

1. Turn the pot upside down to make sure it has drainage holes. If you have a pot that does not have holes, ask an adult to poke a few holes in the bottom with a knife.

2. Fill the pot about two-thirds full with garden earth or potting soil. Place a pot saucer underneath the pot.

3. Ask an adult to help you use the knife to cut a potato into six to eight pieces. Each piece should contain an "eye," a dimpled or indented part of the potato. These eyes actually contain a pointed bud that is the start of a new potato plant root.

4. Arrange the potato pieces on top of the garden earth or potting soil in the pot about 6 to 8 inches (15 to 20 centimeters) apart. Use the ruler to help you measure and space the pieces evenly in the pot.

5. Cover the potato pieces with soil about 5 inches (13 centimeters) deep. Use your hands to gently pat the soil over the potato pieces.

6. Water the soil and place the pot in a sunny spot. Add water regularly to keep the soil moist but not soggy.

7. When the potato plants reach about 4 to 6 inches (10 to 15 centimeters) tall, place a mound of soil over most of the leaves of each plant. This process is called hilling. Hill again in another three weeks.

8. After 90 to 120 days, the flowers on the potato plants will begin to die. This signal means the potatoes are ready to harvest. Dig in the soil to pull up the potatoes.

LIFE IN THE OLD COUNTRY

Healthy potatoes have a light brown skin with small, dented spots called "eyes."

Irish peasants lived in crowded clachan settlements scattered across the countryside. These small communities were not like typical European villages. Clachans had no village square, no shops, and no roads. A group of little homes clustered together made up a clachan.

Irish peasants in a clachan depended on one another. They grew, made, or shared whatever they needed. Many Irish people living in clachans were skilled in trades and could weave cloth, cobble shoes, or thatch roofs. Some of these tradespeople sold their wares to people in England and other nearby European countries.

Peasant families lived in one-room cottages with dirt floors. People rented these simple cottages as well as small plots of land from wealthy landowners. They paid their landowners with part of the crops they grew.

Irish peasants depended on potatoes for their survival. Potatoes were an easy crop to grow in a small space. They required no special tools to plant or harvest. Potatoes did not need to be ground into grain like wheat and corn crops. Potatoes did not quickly spoil, so they could be stored for use throughout the winter.

An Irish cottage had no stove, just a simple hearth for a cooking fire. For fuel, people cut peat blocks from the spongy soil of the Irish bogs and dried them into bricks. They burned these peat bricks and used the fire to boil or roast their potatoes. In the evenings, families sat on the dirt floor around the cooking fire and told stories, recited poems, or sang songs.

Irish peasants often raised a pig or two, and the livestock shared the same living space as the family.

The close-knit Irish people passed their history from one generation to another in the form of stories. They spoke in an ancient Gaelic dialect, which today is called the Irish language. This spoken history included stories of courageous Irish leaders. Many other stories told of St. Patrick, the patron saint of Ireland.

Until the 1500s, Ireland did not have a central government. Most people in Ireland were Catholics. They followed Roman Catholic laws and obeyed priests and other church leaders.

By the 1500s and 1600s, most of the kings and queens who ruled nearby England followed the Protestant faith.

These rulers often sent armies to battle with nearby Catholic countries such as France and Ireland. They gradually conquered land and then replaced the Catholic Irish leaders with English Protestant leaders.

By the 1800s, Ireland was a country of poor peasants who rented land from the English to grow their food. Few families could afford to send their children to school. Each new generation had little hope of making life better than it had been for the last one. At the same time, citizens of England enjoyed an industrial economy and a better standard of living than most Irish. People in England looked on Ireland as a backward country filled with lazy, uneducated peasants.

In 1845, a fungus attacked Irish potato crops. Mold spores grew on potato plant leaves and caused them to turn black and wither. Fresh spores fell off the leaves. Rain washed them into the soil, where they attacked the growing potatoes. Spoiled potatoes developed swollen spots, and the white insides turned soft and yellow. People who ate the spoiled potatoes became sick. Many Irish peasants died from starvation or from eating diseased potatoes.

Spores from the fungus blight lived in the soil and destroyed potatoes in Ireland for five years in a row. The years from 1845 to 1850 were known as the Potato Famine. More than one million Irish peasants died from starvation and disease.

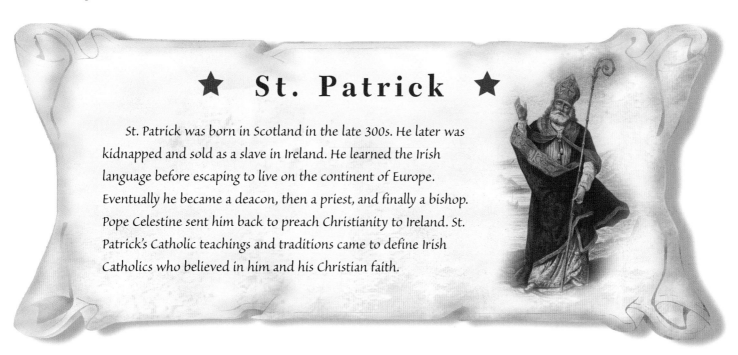

★ St. Patrick ★

St. Patrick was born in Scotland in the late 300s. He later was kidnapped and sold as a slave in Ireland. He learned the Irish language before escaping to live on the continent of Europe. Eventually he became a deacon, then a priest, and finally a bishop. Pope Celestine sent him back to preach Christianity to Ireland. St. Patrick's Catholic teachings and traditions came to define Irish Catholics who believed in him and his Christian faith.

There were no potatoes to eat and no potatoes to pay the rent. When Irish families could not afford to pay the landowner, they had to leave their cottages. Most families had nowhere to go and were too weak from hunger to pack their few belongings. The landlord then would send a constable to evict the tenants. This police officer would force family members out of their cottage and pull down its thatched roof.

Thousands of homeless Irish peasants wandered the Irish countryside. Already weak from hunger, they quickly became infected with disease. Many people died with green stains on their mouths. They were so hungry that they tried to eat green grass, which their sick and empty stomachs could not digest.

About 1.5 million Irish people emigrated to America and Canada during the Potato Famine. Some managed to sell their few possessions to pay for their ship passage. Others had their passage paid by landowners eager to see the starving people leave their land. Most peasants left Ireland in rags. They boarded ships to come to America. Carrying many Irish people weak from disease and starvation, the ships were known as famine ships. Many Irish died during their journey, and the ships also became known as coffin ships.

Some evicted Irish people lived in scalpeens (above). These lean-to shacks were made from the scraps of unroofed cottages. Other families built scalps. They dug holes in the earth about 3 feet (1 meter) deep and covered them with a crude roof of sticks and turf.

THE TRIP OVER

"The next matter . . . was to regulate the allowance of provisions to which each family was entitled, one pound of meal or of bread being allowed for each adult, half a pound for each individual under fourteen years of age, and one-third of a pound for each child under seven years. Thus, although there were 110 souls, great and small, they counted as 84 adults. That was, therefore, the number of pounds to be issued daily."

—Robert Whyte, from The Ocean Plague: The Diary of a Cabin Passenger, *1847*

After landowners began to evict peasants from their homes in the late 1840s, thousands of people suddenly had no place to live, no food to eat, and no hope of finding jobs. They walked from their rural clachan settlements to Dublin and other big cities. More processions of hungry emigrants went to Donegal and Sligo in the north, Limerick and Cork in the southwest, and Waterford and Wexford in the southeast. The ports in these cities offered escape from Ireland.

The Irish emigrants faced more hardships during their journey to America. People who could manage the few dollars for passage boarded cargo ships. These two- or three-masted vessels once had transported cattle. They now carried people. Ship owners quickly built tiny bunks in the steerage section below deck. These berths held sick and weak passengers during the four- to eight-week voyage across the Atlantic Ocean.

Ship owners expected travelers to bring some of their own food and cook it on the steerage stove. But few of the starving peasants had any food to bring. They relied on the supply of food and water stocked on board. The ship's crew gave these food and water rations to passengers a little at a time. But the rations seldom lasted throughout the long journey.

In the late 1840s, during peak famine years, conditions in the steerage sections of cargo ships were at their worst. The ship owners did not spend the time or money to

clean their ships before people boarded.
Workers on a cargo ship first dropped
off a load of supplies from America.
Irish emigrants then quickly crowded
into the dirty spaces that had just held
grain or other supplies.

More passengers died as the
ships became more crowded. Each
passenger had about 2 square feet
(.2 square meter) of space for the
journey. The sleeping areas of these
ships were filthy, crawling with lice
and smelling of foul odors. The
passengers had little food and it often
was spoiled. Many passengers who were
weak with hunger quickly became sick.
About 50,000 Irish people died on the
ships during the journey to America.

Living conditions on ships were crowded
and dirty. So many people died on the
voyages that the vessels carrying Irish
immigrants became known as coffin ships.

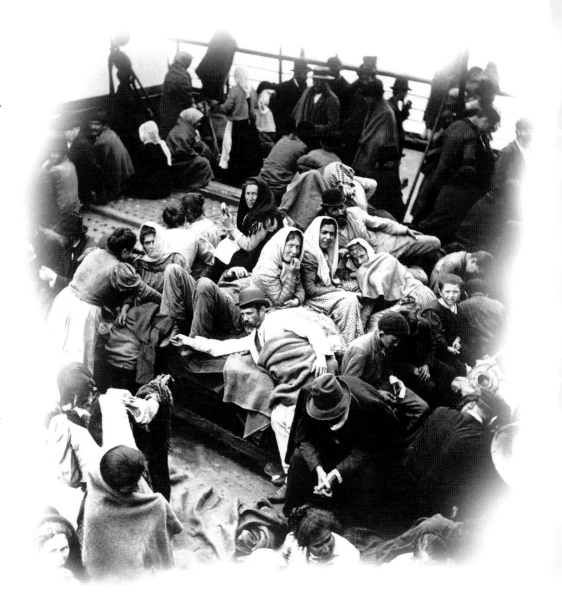

ARRIVING IN AMERICA

From 1855 to 1892, most Irish immigrants entered America through the Castle Garden landing station in New York Harbor. At Castle Garden, ship passengers could find information about jobs and housing. The sickest immigrants received medical attention before entering the country. By the 1890s, the number of immigrants from around the world became too large for Castle Garden to handle. In 1892, Ellis Island opened and became the reception center for the immigrants arriving in New York Harbor.

New York was not the only American destination for Irish immigrants. Many ships sailed to Boston and Philadelphia. New Orleans also was an important port for cotton ships that picked up Irish immigrants during the return trip from Great Britain. The New Orleans port saw the arrival of more Irish immigrants than any other city except New York. Thousands of immigrants settled in the port cities where they landed. But even more traveled across the country on foot or by train in search of work.

As the numbers of famine immigrants piled up in New York and Boston, residents of these cities became alarmed. In a single year, 30,000 immigrants arrived in Boston. The needs of the immigrants were more than the people of the

Irish immigrants found construction work and factory jobs in cities such as New York, Pittsburgh, and Chicago. They built canals in the east and south, and later they laid railroad tracks across the Great Plains of the Midwest.

Irish people crowded into rooming houses called tenements.
The conditions in many tenements were crowded, dark, and
dirty. Several families often shared a single tenement room.

15

Many Irish women found work as domestic servants. They worked as maids cleaning houses or as cooks preparing meals for wealthy families who lived in large cities.

city could supply. At first Bostonians were charitable and helped the immigrants. But as more and more sick and starving immigrants crowded into the city, residents soon grew hostile toward the Irish newcomers.

People began to view the Irish as unfavorable citizens. Newspaper cartoons showed the Irish with ape-like features and usually pictured them fighting or drunk. Many employers would not hire the Irish and posted signs in their shop windows reading, "No Irish Need Apply."

In the 1800s, America had strong Protestant traditions. Many citizens believed the Irish immigrants would be more loyal to the Catholic Church than to America. In some areas of Boston and New York, Irish Catholics began to outnumber the traditional Protestant majority. Angry with the Irish newcomers and their religion, mobs burned Catholic churches in several major cities. The unfavorable feeling toward Irish Catholic immigrants spread to other cities throughout the United States.

★ Irish Soda Bread ★

Irish Soda Bread is one of the best known of the traditional foods brought from Ireland by immigrants in the 1800s. Many Irish servants who earned their living as cooks served this bread to the families who employed them.

What You Need

Ingredients

4 cups (1 liter) all-purpose flour

1 cup (250 mL) sugar

4 teaspoons (20 mL) baking powder

1/2 teaspoon (2 mL) salt

1/2 cup (125 mL) melted butter

1 cup (250 mL) raisins

1 1/2 cups (375 mL) buttermilk

1 egg, lightly beaten

1/2 teaspoon (2 mL) baking soda

1 tablespoon (15 mL) butter, for greasing

Equipment

dry-ingredient measuring cups

measuring spoons

large bowl

wooden spoon

small bowl

paper towel or napkin

large cast-iron or oven-proof
   frying pan

knife

What You Do

1. Preheat oven to 375°F (190° C).

2. Mix flour, sugar, baking powder, and salt together in a large bowl.

3. Add melted butter. Stir well with wooden spoon.

4. Stir raisins into ingredients in bowl.

5. In a small bowl, combine buttermilk, 1 lightly beaten egg, and baking soda.

6. Use the wooden spoon to make a dip in the center of the batter in the large bowl. Pour the ingredients from the small bowl into the dip in the batter. Stir ingredients together with the wooden spoon to form bread dough.

7. Dab butter with a paper towel or napkin and grease the large cast-iron or oven-proof frying pan.

8. Place the dough into the greased pan. Use a knife to cut a cross design on the top of the dough.

9. Bake the bread for one hour, until the top is golden brown.

10. Cut into wedges and serve warm from the pan.

Serves 6 to 8

OUR COUNTRY AND HER FLAG.

NATIVE

AMERICANS.

Published & for Sale by W. L. Germon.
215 Chesnut St. 2nd door above 7th
Philadelphia.

By the 1850s, some people were so angry and suspicious of the Irish that they started a new political movement. The "Know Nothing" party was a group of people officially known as the American Party. They opposed immigration and supported slavery. The group did not believe in treating all people fairly and they wanted to keep their actions secret. When someone asked a member about the group's beliefs or actions, the person said, "I know nothing." Members did not want to reveal anything about the group. The Know Nothings held a majority in a number of state governments and wanted to limit these political offices to native-born American citizens. In several states, the Know Nothing members helped pass anti-Catholic laws that denied voting rights to immigrants.

The unfair treatment they first received in America made the Irish people stick together. With no one to help them, the immigrants helped one another. They lived close together and shared what they had. An Irish woman who worked in the kitchen of a wealthy family might try to get a job for a friend at the same house. Irish men also helped fellow immigrants find work. Irish children protected their younger brothers and sisters from bullies who mocked and teased them for being poor. Irish immigrants gradually gained political power by supporting candidates who were sympathetic to their problems. Irish Americans became expert political organizers.

Unjust attitudes against Irish Catholics lingered long after the Civil War (1861–1865), but Irish Americans earned respect for their political and labor union power. Workers joined together to demand better wages and working conditions. Groups of workers formed unions, agreeing to strike by stopping work until their employers made needed changes. Just the threat of a union strike sometimes was enough to make changes the workers wanted.

This 1844 Know Nothing Party campaign ribbon contains patriotic images such as the American flag and George Washington. But the Know Nothings sometimes committed acts of violence to scare immigrants out of the country.

Irish immigrants were among the soldiers who fought in the Civil War. Their reputation for courage in battle earned respect from soldiers of other nationalities.

SURVIVING IN AMERICA

Clothing mills hired Irish children to fill jobs in the factory, such as feeding thread into textile machines.

To be able to survive in America, Irish immigrants had to find jobs. Most Irish Americans were uneducated and unskilled. The men were willing to perform manual labor for low wages. The women found jobs cooking and cleaning for wealthy families. Children worked at home making lace, or found jobs operating machinery in cotton mills and other factories.

In the late 1800s, America needed thousands of laborers to build railroads to the West. Irish men were among the many laborers who dug ditches, moved rocks, and laid railroad ties. The men worked in hot, humid weather using shovels to dig by hand.

Thousands of Irish women worked as household servants for wealthy families in New York, Boston, Philadelphia, and New Orleans. So many Irish women made their living as domestics that the common Irish name Bridgid was used to refer to any servant girl. These women played an important role in Irish immigration. They saved their wages and sent money back to Ireland to bring family members to America. By the late 1800s, Irish American women had earned most of the money that paid for Irish immigration from 1900 to 1920.

Some Irish immigrant women found jobs in the factories of America's large cities. They earned $1 a day working long hours as seamstresses in the clothing mills of Massachusetts. Their jobs were dangerous because the machines gave off fumes that made breathing difficult. Fires often started in the dusty factory buildings.

The Irish were the first immigrant group to establish Catholicism as a major faith in America. Irish immigrants depended on the Catholic Church for advice and guidance as well as for food and medical attention. The local priest was a well-respected member of the Irish community. Parishioners often appealed to the priest for assistance in finding a job, settling an argument, or punishing a child. Women who belonged to religious orders ran schools and hospitals. These nuns never turned away a student or a patient because of their background, their income, or their social standing.

Some ambitious Irish immigrants moved west. Many joined the Gold Rush of 1849 after miners discovered gold in the hills of California. Some Irish Americans struck it rich. John Mackie mined for gold in the famous Comstock Lode outside Virginia City, Nevada. Through hard work, he made his way from laborer to superintendent of the mine. By the 1870s, Mackie was one of the richest men in America.

In the 1880s, the invention of electricity created a huge demand for copper wiring. Marcus Daly, another Irish immigrant, worked his way up to the head of a huge copper mining operation in Butte, Montana. The Anaconda Copper Mine became one of the most successful mining operations in the country. Daly was

Mining companies hired Irish children to work long hours in the mines. The work was dangerous and labor unions fought to stop the practice of hiring children.

21

"This factory was run also by child labor. Here, too, were the children running up and down between the spindles. The lint was heavy in the room. The machinery needed constant cleaning. The tiny, slender bodies of the little children crawled in and about under dangerous machinery, oiling and cleaning. Often their hands were crushed. A finger was snapped off."

—Mary Harris "Mother" Jones, labor union leader, 1925

more generous with his workers than most mine owners, perhaps because he employed so many Irish immigrants. If a miner was killed in an Anaconda mine, Daly provided the man's widow with a brand-new brick house.

Butte had the highest percentage of Irish-born residents of any community in America. Many of the immigrant miners in Butte still spoke their Gaelic language both at home and around town. St. Patrick's Day parades and Irish wakes were part of the Butte community's Irish identity. Miners' Union Day on June 13 was an equally important holiday and one of the only days of the year that the Anaconda mine was closed.

Most Irish American workers were not as lucky as the Anaconda miners. Irish immigrant workers usually were hired for the dirtiest and most dangerous jobs an employer had to offer. To fight back, Irish workers organized unions to fight terrible working conditions and low wages paid to Irish workers. By the 1880s, Irish leaders ran half the labor unions in America.

As Irish Americans prospered they became more involved in American politics. In New York, the strong Irish community joined Tammany Hall, the state's major Democratic Party organization. Irish immigrants won jobs and power in city government through political organizing. By the 1890s, many Irish Americans held city jobs, often working as police officers and fire fighters.

★ Tammany Hall ★

By the late 1840s, Irish immigrants had put their political skills to work at New York's Tammany Hall. Founded in 1789, this group was the management committee of New York's Democratic Party. At first, only Protestant working men were allowed to join. Catholics could not become members. But thousands of Irish immigrants registered as Democrats and demanded to be included in Tammany Hall.

Irish Americans rallied behind Mike Walsh, a journalist born in County Cork and raised in New York. He founded a newspaper for the city's poor working classes. He also was noted for his ability as a public speaker. By the time of Walsh's death in 1859, his group of Irish followers was running Tammany Hall. They reigned at the top of Democratic Party politics through the end of the 1800s.

KEEPING TRADITIONS

Leaves of the oxalis plant often are called shamrocks. St. Patrick is said to have used the three leaves of a shamrock to teach about the Holy Trinity.

Irish American unity helped the immigrants achieve success in America. They formed labor unions, political groups, and social organizations such as Hibernian societies. In 1565, the Ancient Order of Hibernians began in Ireland. This was the first Catholic fraternal organization. It was formed to preserve Irish traditions and values. In 1836, Irish Americans formed their own Hibernian Society in New York. It is the oldest Catholic fraternal organization in the United States. Hibernian Societies have formed in many other U.S. cities as well.

St. Patrick's Day, on March 17, has a long tradition in the United States. Irish Americans celebrate their heritage on this day. Parades with shamrock-adorned floats, kilt-wearing bagpipers, and Irish folk dancers wind down main streets in most major cities. People shout "Erin Go Braugh," which means "Ireland Forever."

The largest St. Patrick's Day parade is in New York City, where the greatest number of Irish Americans live today. More than two million people attend New York's annual St. Patrick's Day parade. Many other U.S. cities have St. Patrick's Day parades and celebrations, including Chicago, Baltimore, Boston, Omaha, St. Paul, and Dallas.

On St. Patrick's Day and at other celebrations, the sounds of ringing strings from the Celtic harp can be heard. Smaller than pedal harps, Celtic harps are lightweight and portable. Many modern musical groups use the small harp in their arrangements.

The Clancy Brothers made Irish ballads a popular form of music. A ballad is a kind of musical poem that tells a story. The Clancy Brothers were a popular folk group in the 1960s. They were known for their whoops, whistles, and leg-slaps while they performed on stage.

Step-dancing has undergone many changes since Irish immigrants first brought it to America. The jig and the reel were the earliest forms of Irish dance. Both of these dances combine fast and lively steps to music. In 1995, the dance production *Riverdance* brought new attention to this traditional form of Irish dancing.

Irish food, clothing, and jewelry are popular in America. Most large American cities have Irish pubs that offer traditional meals, such as shepherd's pie. In gift stores, Irish customers can buy traditional Aran

In Chicago on St. Patrick's Day, members of a local pipefitters union dye the Chicago River green.

Claddagh ring

sweaters made in Ireland. Sometimes called fisherman knit, these wool sweaters are made with twisted stitches and have fancy raised designs. Many Irish Americans wear a Claddagh ring, a tradition that began in a small fishing village near Galway in Ireland. The ring has a design that combines a heart, a pair of hands, and a crown. Irish tradition says that the heart symbolizes love, the hands stand for friendship, and the crown means loyalty.

Irish people continue to immigrate to America. But the number of new Irish immigrants began to decline after 1921, when Ireland won independence from Great Britain. Independence brought hope to the Irish for a better life in their homeland.

In 1960, Irish American John F. Kennedy was elected the 35th U.S. president. He was not the first president of Irish heritage, but he was the first Catholic president and the youngest man to be elected to the country's highest office. Kennedy's presidency was a signal to many Irish Americans that the descendants of poor, starving peasants from Ireland had finally been accepted into American culture.

St. Patrick's Cathedral in New York has been recognized as a center of Catholic life in America since 1879.

26

★ Make a Family Tree ★

Genealogy is the study of family history. Genealogists often record this history in the form of a family tree. This chart records a person's ancestors, such as parents, grandparents, and great-grandparents.

Start your own family tree with the names of your parents and grandparents. Ask family members for their full names, including their middle names. Remember that your mother and grandmothers likely had a different last name before they were married. This name, called a maiden name, is probably the same as their fathers' last name.

Making a family tree helps you to know your ancestors and the countries from which they emigrated. Some people include the dates and places of birth with each name on their family tree. Knowing when and where these relatives were born will help you understand from which immigrant groups you have descended.

There are many ways to find information for your family tree. Ask for information from your parents, grandparents, and as many other older members of your family as you can. Some people research official birth and death records to find the full names of relatives. Genealogical societies often have information that will help with family tree research. If you know the cemetery where family members are buried, you may find some of the information you need on the gravestones.

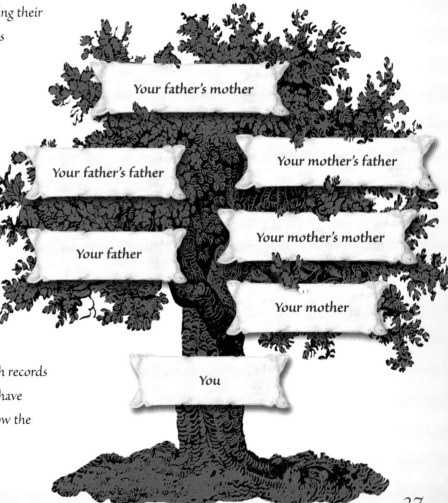

Your father's mother

Your mother's father

Your father's father

Your mother's mother

Your father

Your mother

You

★ TIMELINE ★

1914
World War I begins.
The first Irish Home Rule
bill, which calls for an
independent government
of Ireland, passes in the
British House of Lords.
But the bill does not go
into effect until the end of
the war.

1854
Protesters stage violent
demonstrations against
Irish immigrants in
several U.S. cities.

1845-1849
Blight destroys Ireland's potato
crop, resulting in widespread
famine across the Irish
countryside. One million Irish
people die and one-third of the
Irish population emigrates.

1735
The oldest Irish group
in the United States,
the Charitable Irish
Society, is founded.

1700

1800

1900

1759
The first
St. Patrick's Day
parade is staged in
New York City.

1849
California's gold rush
draws thousands of Irish
immigrants to California.

1920
Irish Americans make up
more than 31 percent of
Boston's population.

1922
Ireland is divided into
two countries. Northern
Ireland becomes part of
Great Britain. The larger,
southern part becomes an
independent country
called the Republic
of Ireland.

1801
Ireland becomes a
part of Great Britain
through passage of
the Act of Union.

1861-1865
Thousands of Irish
Americans join
the Union or
Confederate armies
and fight in the
Civil War.

1897
The Irish American
Historical Society is
founded in Boston.

★ **Buffalo Bill Cody** (1846–1917) Cody was a pony express rider, Indian scout, and buffalo hunter. Cody organized *Buffalo Bill's Wild West Show*, with attractions such as a Pony Express relay race and Custer's Last Fight. The show was an international success, touring throughout the United States and Europe.

★ **Henry Ford** (1863–1947) Ford was an inventor and a businessman. He started the Ford Motor Company in 1903. Ford invented the assembly line to build cars. This method made cars more affordable to the greatest number of people. By 1918, half of all cars in America were Ford's Model Ts.

★ **Judy Garland** (1922–1969) Born Frances Ethel Gumm, she starred in many movies, including *The Wizard of Oz*. The song "It's a Great Day for the Irish" was written especially for Judy Garland. It was one of the longest-selling musical hits from 1941 to 1980.

Judy Garland

★ **John F. Kennedy** (1917–1963) Kennedy served in the U.S. Navy during World War II (1939-1945). Later, he became a Congressman from the Boston area, and in 1953 was elected to the U.S. Senate. Kennedy became the 35th president in 1960. He was assassinated in Dallas, Texas, in 1963. Kennedy was the youngest man elected president, as well as the youngest president to die in office.

★ **Bill Murray** (1950–) A well-known comedy actor, Murray entertained TV viewers on the *Saturday Night Live* show from 1977 to 1980. He also has starred in the movies *Caddyshack*, *Ghostbusters*, and *Scrooged*.

John F. Kennedy

29

Words to Know

achieve (uh-CHEEV)—to do something successfully, especially after a lot of effort

Celtic (KEL-tik)—belonging to a group of people from western Ireland

dialect (DYE-uh-lekt)—a way a language is spoken in a particular place or among a particular group of people

emigrate (EM-uh-grate)—to leave your own country in order to live in another one

evict (ee-VIKT)—to force people to move out of their homes

fraternal (frah-TIR-nuhl)—a society or organization to which only men belong

genealogy (jee-nee-AL-uh-jee)—the study of family history

heritage (HER-uh-tij)—valuable or important traditions handed down from generation to generation

immigrant (IM-uh-gruhnt)—someone who comes from abroad to live permanently in a country

spore (SPOR)—a plant cell that grows into a new plant; spores are produced by plants that do not flower, such as fungi, mosses, and ferns.

thatch (THACH)—a roof covering made from straw or reeds

tradition (truh-DISH-uhn)—the handing down of customs, ideas, and beliefs from one generation to the next

To Learn More

Bunting, Eve. *Dreaming of America: An Ellis Island Story.* Mahwah, N.J.: Bridge Water Books, 1999.

Coffey, Michael, Ed., and text by Terry Golway. *The Irish in America.* New York: Hyperion, 1997.

Hoobler, Dorothy, and Thomas Hoobler. *The Irish American Family Album.* American Family Albums. New York: Oxford University Press, 1998.

Laxton, Edward. *The Famine Ships: The Irish Exodus to America, 1846-1851.* New York: Henry Holt, 1997.

Places to Write and Visit

American Irish Historical Society
991 Fifth Avenue
New York, NY 10028

Ellis Island Library
Statue of Liberty National Monument
1 Liberty Island
New York, NY 10004

Grosse Île and the Irish Memorial National Historic Site
2 D'Auteuil Street
P.O. Box 2474, Postal Terminal
Québec, QC
G1K 7R3 Canada

Irish American Cultural Institute
1 Lackawanna Place
Morristown, NJ 07960

Irish Immigration Center
59 Temple Place, Suite 1105
Boston, MA 02111

The National Genealogical Society
4527 17th Street North
Arlington, VA 22207-2399

Internet Sites

Boston Family History
http://www.bostonfamilyhistory.com

Interpreting the Irish Famine, 1845–1850
http://www.people.virginia.edu/~eas5e/Irish/Famine.html

Irish Immigration Center
http://www.iicenter.org

Old Irish-Gaelic Surnames
http://www.fortunecity.com/bally/kilkenny/2/irenames.htm

A Scattering of Seeds: The Creation of Canada, Irish Immigration
http://www.whitepinepictures.com/seeds/series1/episode-0121/history.html

Views of the Famine
http://vassun.vassar.edu/~sttaylor/FAMINE

Index